The Day the Humans Stayed Home

A Quarantine Tail

Written by
Aimee Wood

Illustrated by
Amanda Haack

Leaning Rock Press

Copyright © 2021 Aimee Wood and Amanda Haack

All rights reserved. No parts of this publication may be reproduced, stored in a database or retrieval system, or transmitted, in any form or by any means, without the prior permission of the author or publisher, except by a reviewer who may quote brief passages in a review.

Leaning Rock Press
Gales Ferry, CT 06335
leaningrockpress@gmail.com
www.leaningrockpress.com

978-1-950323-43-2, Hardcover
978-1-950323-44-9, Softcover

Library of Congress Control Number: 2021905347

Publisher's Cataloging-In-Publication Data
(Prepared by The Donohue Group, Inc.)

Names: Wood, Aimee, author. | Haack, Amanda, illustrator.
Title: The day the humans stayed home : a quarantine tail / written by Aimee Wood ; illustrated by Amanda Haack.
Description: Gales Ferry, CT : Leaning Rock Press, [2021] | Interest age level: 003-008. | Summary: Travel through a day in the life of Homer the dog when life as he knew it comes to a halt. Due to the coronavirus pandemic, Homer experiences many changes alongside his human companions. He also realizes his value in comforting his human companions.
Identifiers: ISBN 9781950323432 (hardcover) | ISBN 9781950323449 (softcover)
Subjects: LCSH: Quarantine--Psychological aspects--Juvenile fiction. | COVID-19 (Disease)--Social aspects--Juvenile fiction. | Dogs--Juvenile fiction. | Human-animal relationships--Juvenile fiction. | CYAC: Quarantine--Psychological aspects--Fiction. | COVID-19 (Disease)--Social aspects--Fiction. | Dogs--Fiction. | Human-animal relationships--Fiction
Classification: LCC PZ7.1.W646 Da 2021d | DDC [E]--dc23

Printed in the United States of America

First, I would like to say thank you to my friends and
family,
who supported me throughout the process of
publishing this book.
Without you, this wouldn't have gotten done.

Also, this goes out to all the essential workers,
including my fellow educators,
for your dedication and commitment throughout
the pandemic.
We are all in this together.

Finally, to my pandemic buddy, Homer,
my four-legged companion.

Hi. My name is Homer!
My life changed before I knew it
back in March of 2020.

I had gotten used to my humans
leaving for the day.

I always missed them, but I had a pretty full day.
I'd look out the window,
test the couch's durability,

check the safety of the humans' bed,
scratch, nap, eat, drink and repeat.

Every day around 3:30
I had to protect my humans' home from
that mail carrier, as they called him.
Mom said he was bad because
all she ever got was bills.

I let him know that this was my home,
and he would agree and leave me a treat.
So, I let him walk away in peace.

Then around 4:30
my humans came home!

There were plenty of belly scratches,
a long walk, and a full bowl of dinner.
Life was good.

Then one day,
life changed,
and the humans stayed home.

We watched a lot of news those first few days.
There was lots of talk about a virus,
The Coronavirus, and a pandemic.

The humans took over my couches.

They took back their beds.

They didn't let me tell that mail carrier whose house this was!

Then there was a new
person I needed to
protect my humans
from, but she brought
our food
so I thought
she must be okay.

Everywhere I went in the house,
the humans were there.

They insisted we go on multiple walks a day.

And I was TIRED!

What was this coronavirus?
Little germs that could make my humans sick.

They needed to stay home to keep us safe.
They cleaned A LOT and
they had to wear masks when they went out.

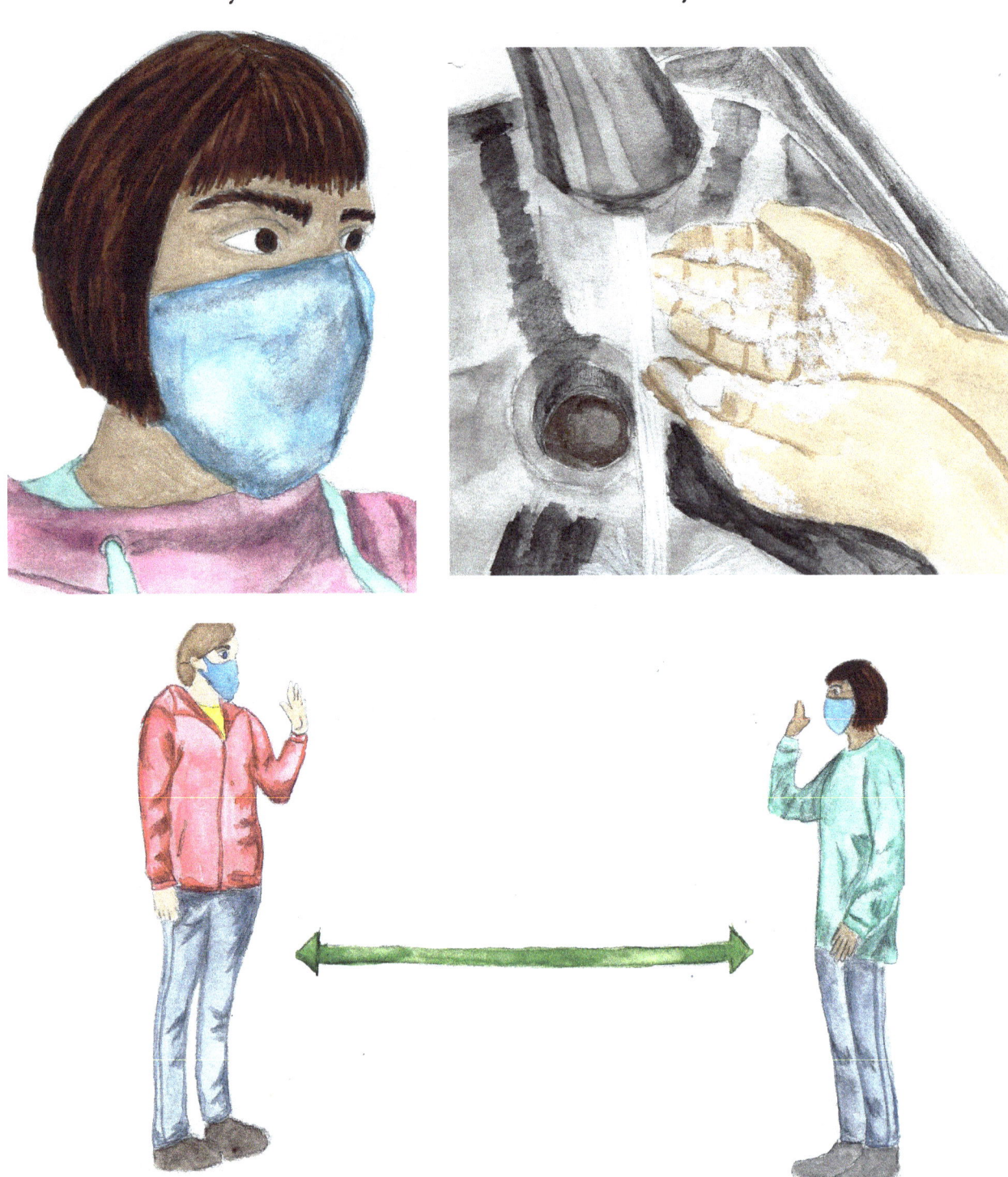

This went on for MONTHS!

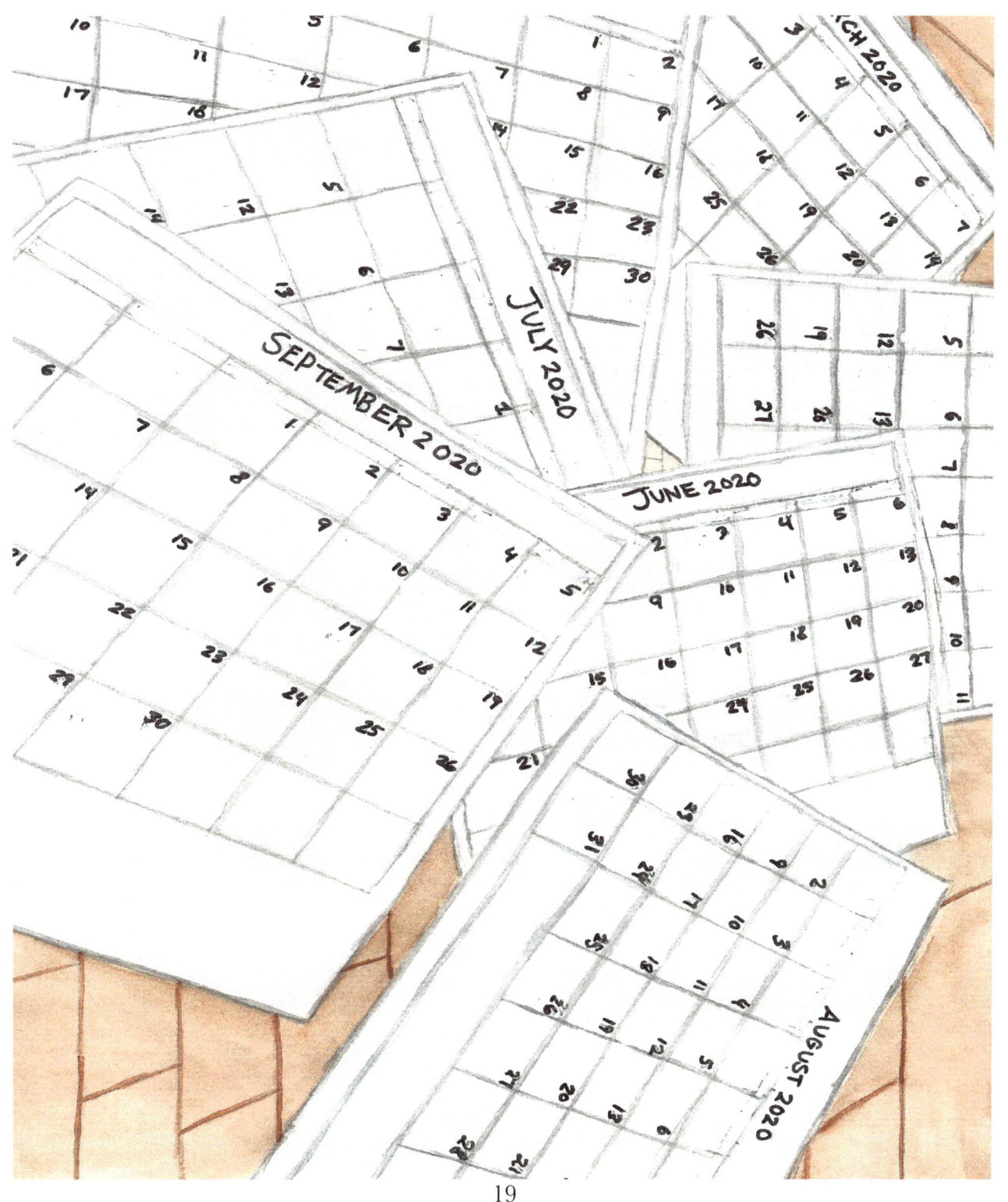

I could see that my humans needed a little extra love,
so I didn't mind the snuggles.

I was very upset when Grandma couldn't visit,
but we talked to her through the little human TV.

It was hard.
We didn't see my dog friends like we used to,
and my humans couldn't see their companions as much either.

But you know what?
We started to make baskets of goodies for people and left them on their doorsteps so they could feel happy.

We got to talk to other humans and even my canine friends through something called zoom.

I let the mail carrier off easy
because he took and brought the letters we wrote to friends.
I would sign them with my paw prints.

I started to not mind all the walks.
Exercise was good for my humans to keep them healthy.

They even bought me my own bed for naps.

Life was not as it had been, but the humans got to slow down, and that was good for them.

Life was certainly different,
but we realized we had so much to be thankful for.

If this virus taught us anything,
it was to believe in the power of kindness.

Appreciate those who care for and love you.

Most importantly,
we can get through anything
as long as we have each other.

And now I have a whole new appreciation
for those quiet times at home
when my humans went back to work.

Author
Aimee Wood

Aimee Wood is a teacher from New London, CT. She studied Athletic Training and Sport Management at Mitchell College, earning two degrees before receiving her teacher's certification from Charter Oak State College. She is currently teaching pre-kindergarten at The Friendship School in Waterford, CT, and is currently pursuing a Master's Degree in Special Education. When she is not teaching, she enjoys writing, drawing, painting, being outside, playing softball and football, and being an Auntie. *The Day the Humans Stayed Home* is her first children's book, and she hopes to publish more.

Illustrator
Amanda Haack

Amanda Haack has held various positions at Regional Multicultural Magnet School in New London since 2012. In the last few years, she has worked as a Substitute teacher and Enrichment Presenter. Originally from the Buckeye State in Toledo, Ohio. She earned her Bachelor's degree in Two-Dimensional Art at Bowling Green State University. When Amanda is not at the school, she is creating new projects, reading, cuddling with her pets Nutmeg (dog) and Ichabod (cat). The Day the Humans Stayed Home is the first book she has illustrated, and she hopes there are many more books in the future.

CPSIA information can be obtained
at www.ICGtesting.com
Printed in the USA
LVHW050711160421
684556LV00002B/34